LUTHER's
SMALL
CATECHISM

GREAT CHRISTIAN BOOKS
LINDENHURST, NEW YORK

LUTHER's
SMALL
CATECHISM

A GREAT CHRISTIAN BOOKS publication
Great Christian Books is an imprint of Rotolo Media
160 37th Street Lindenhurst, New York 11757
www.GreatChristianBooks.com   (631) 956-0998
email: mail@greatchristianbooks.com
Luther's Small Catechism
ISBN 978-1-61010-166-0

Luther, Martin, 1483-1546
Luther's Small Catechism / by Martin Luther
p. cm.
A "A Great Christian Book" book
GREAT CHRISTIAN BOOKS an imprint of Rotolo Media
ISBN 978-1-61010-166-0
Dewey Decimal Classifications: 200, 238
Suggested Subject Headings:
1. Religion—Christian literature—Christianity &
Christian theology
2. Christianity—The Bible—Creeds & Catechisms
I. Title

Book and cover design for this title are by Michael Rotolo.
Body text is typeset in the Minion typeface by Adobe Inc. and
is quality manufactured in the United States on acid-free paper.
To discuss the publication of your Christian manuscript or out-
of-print book, please contact Great Christian Books.

CONTENTS

LUTHER'S PREFACE TO THE SMALL CATECHISM

Martin Luther, to all faithful and godly pastors and preachers: grace, mercy, and peace be yours in Jesus Christ, our Lord.

The deplorable, miserable conditions which I recently observed when visiting the parishes have constrained and pressed me to put this catechism of Christian doctrine into this brief, plain, and simple form. How pitiable, so help me God, were the things I saw: the common man, especially in the villages, knows practically nothing of Christian doctrine, and many of the pastors are almost entirely incompetent and unable to teach. Yet all the people are supposed to be Christians, have been baptized, and receive the Holy Sacrament even though they do not know the Lord's Prayer, the Creed, or the Ten Commandments and live like poor animals of the barnyard and pigpen. What these people have mastered, however, is the fine art of tearing all Christian liberty to shreds.

Oh, you bishops! How will you ever answer to Christ for letting the people carry on so disgracefully and not attending to the duties of your office even for a moment? One can only hope judgment does not strike you! You command the Sacrament in one kind only, insist on the observance of your human ways, and yet are unconcerned whether the people know the Lord's Prayer, the Creed, the Ten Commandments, or indeed any of God's Word. Woe, woe to you forever!

Therefore dear brothers, for God's sake I beg all of you who are pastors and preachers to devote yourselves sincerely to the duties of your office, that you feel compassion for the people entrusted to your care, and that you help us accordingly to inculcate this catechism in the people, especially the young. If you cannot do more, at least take the tables and charts for catechism instruction and drill the people in them word for word, in the following way:

First, the pastor should most carefully avoid teaching the Ten Commandments, the Lord's Prayer, the Creed, the sacraments, etc., according to various texts and differing forms. Let him adopt one version, stay with it, and from one year to the next keep using it unchanged. Young and inexperienced persons must be taught a single fixed form or they will easily become confused, and the result will be that all previous effort and labor will be lost. There should be no change, even though one may wish to improve the text.

The honored fathers understood this well, and therefore they all consistently used one form of the Lord's Prayer, the Creed, and the Ten Commandments. We should do as they did by teaching these materials to the young and the common man without altering a single syllable and by never varying their wording when presenting or quoting them year after year.

So adopt whatever form you wish, and then stick with it at all times. If, however, you happen to be preaching to some sophisticated, learned audience, then you certainly may demonstrate your skill with words by turning phrases as colorfully and masterfully as you can. But with young persons keep to a single, fixed, and permanent form and wording, and teach them first of all the Ten Commandments, the Creed, the Lord's Prayer, etc according to the text, word for word, so that can repeat it after you and commit it to memory.

But those who refuse to learn are to be told that they are denying Christ and do not belong to Him. They are not to be admitted to the

Sacrament, accepted as sponsors at Baptism, or allowed to exercise Christian liberty in any way. They should instead be simply directed back to the pope and his functionaries, yes, even to Satan himself. Moreover, their parents and superiors should refuse them food and drink, telling them that the prince is of a mind to expel such rude persons from his realm, and so on.

Of course we cannot, and we should not try to, force the Christian faith on anyone. Yet we should steadily keep on urging people toward it and help them know what is considered right and wrong in the society in which they want to live and earn their living. A person who wants to live in a certain city and enjoy its privileges should know and observe its laws, no matter whether he believes in them or is at heart a rogue or scoundrel.

Second, after they have well memorized the text (of the catechism), then explain the meaning so that they understand what they are saying. Do so again with the help of these charts or some other brief uniform method of your choosing; adhere to it and do not change a single syllable, as said above concerning the text, taking your time with it. For it is not necessary to teach everything at once, but one thing after the other. After they understand well the meaning of the First Commandment, proceed to the Second, and so on, otherwise they will be too overwhelmed to the point of remembering nothing.

Third, after you have so taught them this short catechism, take up the Large Catechism and use it to give them a broader and richer understanding. Here enlarge on every individual commandment, petition, segment, explaining in each case the various words, uses, benefits, dangers, and hurts involved, as you will find them amply described in many a book dealing with these topics. Stress especially that commandment or any other specific part of the catechism doctrine which your people neglect most. For example, among craftsmen and merchants, farmers and employees, you must powerfully stress the Seventh Commandment, which forbids stealing, because among such people many kinds of dishonesty and thievery occur. Also, for young persons and the common man you must stress the Fourth Commandment, urging them to be orderly, faithful, obedient, and peaceable, always bringing in many Bible examples of how God punished or blessed such people.

You should particularly urge those in authority and parents to govern the young well and to send them to school. Show them why it is their duty to do this and explain what a damnable sin it is if they fail to do so. For by such neglect they ruin and destroy both the kingdom of God and that of this world and prove themselves to be the worst enemies of both God and man. Thoroughly underscore what terrible harm they do by not helping train children to become pastors, preachers, writers, and the like, and how God will punish them for it. There is a great need to preach about these things. For parents and those in authority are guilty beyond words in this regard, and the devil has horrible things in mind.

Finally, now that the pope's tyranny is over, people no longer want to go to the Sacrament but despise it. Here again urging is necessary, however, with the understanding that we are not to force anyone into the faith or to the Sacrament, nor set any law, time, or place for it. Our preaching should instead be such that of their own accord and without our command, people feel constrained themselves and press us pastors to serve the Sacrament. The way to go about this is to tell them that if anyone does not seek or desire the Lord's Supper at the very least four times a year, it is to be feared that he despises the Sacrament and is not Christian, just as no one is a Christian who does not believe or hear the Gospel. For Christ did not say, "Omit this" or "despise this," but "This do, as often as you drink it," etc. He most certainly wants it done and does not want it left undone and despised. "This do," He says.

For a person not to prize highly the Sacrament is tantamount to saying that he has no sin, no flesh, no devil, no world, no death, no danger, no hell. That is to say, he believes in none of these although he is overwhelmed by them and is the devil's possession twice over. On the other hand, he needs no grace, life, paradise, kingdom of heaven, Christ, God, or any good thing. Surely, if he recognized how much evil is in him and how much he needs all the good things he lacks, he would not neglect the Sacrament, which gives help against such evil and bestows so much goodness. He will not need to be forced by law to the Sacrament but will himself come running in a hurry to the Lord's Table, constrained within himself and pressing you to give him the Sacrament.

Therefore do not set up any law concerning it, as the pope does. Only emphasize clearly the benefit, need, usefulness, and blessing connected with the Sacrament, and also the harm and danger of neglecting it. The people will then come of themselves without your using compulsion. But if they still do not come, then let them go their way and tell them that all who are insensitive or unaware of their great need and God's gracious help belong to the devil. But if you fail to urge these things or if you make it into law and bitterness, then the fault will be yours if they despise the Sacrament. Why should they not be lazy if you are asleep and silent?

So look to it, you pastors and preachers. Our ministry today is something else than it was under the pope. It has become a serious and saving responsibility. Consequently it now involves much more trouble and labor, danger and trial, and in addition it brings you little of the world's gratitude and rewards. But Christ Himself will be our reward if we labor faithfully. The Father of all grace help us to do just that. To Him be praise and thanks forever through Christ our Lord. Amen.

SECTION 1

THE TEN COMMANDMENTS*

THE HEAD OF THE FAMILY SHOULD TEACH
IT IN A SIMPLE WAY TO HIS HOUSEHOLD.

The First Commandment

You shall have no other gods.

Q. *What does this mean?*

A. We should fear, love, and trust in God above all things.

The Second Commandment

You shall not misuse the name of the Lord your God.

Q. *What does this mean?*

A. We should fear and love God so that we do not curse, swear, use satanic arts, lie, or deceive by His name, but call upon it in every trouble, pray, praise, and give thanks.

---

*The text of the commandments is from Ex. 20:3, 7, 8, 12–17.

The Third Commandment

You shall sanctify the holy day. [Remember the Sabbath day by keeping it holy.]

Q. *What does this mean?*

A. We should fear and love God so that we do not despise preaching and His Word, but hold it sacred and gladly hear and learn it.

The Fourth Commandment

Honour your father and your mother.

Q. *What does this mean?*

A. We should fear and love God so that we do not despise or anger our parents and other authorities, but honour them, serve and obey them, love and cherish them.

The Fifth Commandment

You shall not murder.

Q. *What does this mean?*

A. We should fear and love God so that we do not hurt or harm our neighbour in his body, but help and support him in every physical need.

The Sixth Commandment

You shall not commit adultery.

Q. *What does this mean?*

A. We should fear and love God so that we

lead a sexually pure and decent life in what we say and do, and husband and wife love and honour each other.

The Seventh Commandment

You shall not steal.

Q. *What does this mean?*

A. We should fear and love God so that we do not take our neighbour's money or possessions, or get them in any dishonest way, but help him to improve and protect his possessions and income.

The Eighth Commandment

You shall not give false testimony against your neighbour.

Q. *What does this mean?*

A. We should fear and love God so that we do not tell lies about our neighbour, betray him, slander him, or hurt his reputation, but defend him, speak well of him, and explain everything in the kindest way.

The Ninth Commandment

You shall not covet your neighbour's house.

Q. *What does this mean?*

A. We should fear and love God so that we do not scheme to get our neighbour's inheritance or house, or get it in a way which only appears right, but help and be of service to him in keeping it.

The Tenth Commandment

You shall not covet your neighbour's wife, or his manservant or maidservant, his ox or donkey, or anything that belongs to your neighbour.

Q. *What does this mean?*

A. We should fear and love God so that we do not entice or force away our neighbour's wife, workers, or animals, or turn them against him, but urge them to stay and do their duty.

The Close of the Commandments

What does God say about all these commandments?

A. He says—

"I, the Lord your God, am a jealous God, punishing the children for the sin of the fathers to the third and fourth generation of those who hate Me, but showing love to a thousand generations of those who love Me and keep My command-ments." —Ex. 20:5-6

Q. *What does this mean?*

A. God threatens to punish all who break these commandments. Therefore, we should fear His wrath and not do anything against them. But He promises grace and every blessing to all who keep these commandments. Therefore, we should also love and trust in Him and gladly do what He commands.

THE CREED

The First Article

CREATION

I believe in God, the Father Almighty, Maker of heaven and earth.

Q. *What does this mean?*

A. I believe that God has made me and all creatures; that He has given me my body and soul, eyes, ears, and all my members, my reason and all my senses, and still takes care of them.

He also gives me clothing and shoes, food and drink, house and home, wife and children, land, animals, and all I have. He richly and daily provides me with all that I need to support this body and life.

He defends me against all danger and guards and protects me from all evil.

All this He does only out of fatherly, divine goodness and mercy, without any merit or worthiness in me. For all this it is my duty to thank and praise, serve and obey Him.

This is most certainly true.

The Second Article

REDEMPTION

And in Jesus Christ, His only Son, our Lord, who was conceived by the Holy Spirit, born of the Virgin Mary, suffered under Pontius Pilate, was crucified, died and was buried. He descended into hell. The third day He rose again from the dead. He ascended into heaven and sits at the right hand of God, the Father Almighty. From thence He will come to judge the living and the dead.

Q. *What does this mean?*

A. I believe that Jesus Christ, true God, begotten of the Father from eternity, and also true man, born of the Virgin Mary, is my Lord, who has redeemed me, a lost and condemned person, purchased and won me from all sins, from death, and from the power of the devil; not with gold or silver, but with His holy, precious blood and with His innocent suffering and death, that I may be His own and live under Him in His kingdom and serve Him in everlasting righteousness, innocence, and blessedness, just as He is risen from the dead, lives and reigns to all eternity. This is most certainly true.

The Third Article

SANCTIFICATION

I believe in the Holy Spirit, the holy Christian church, the communion of saints, the forgiveness of sins, the resurrection of the body, and the life everlasting. Amen.

Q. *What does this mean?*

A. I believe that I cannot by my own reason or strength believe in Jesus Christ, my Lord, or come to Him; but the Holy Spirit has called me by the Gospel, enlightened me with His gifts, sanctified and kept me in the true faith.

In the same way He calls, gathers, enlightens, and sanctifies the whole Christian church on earth, and keeps it with Jesus Christ in the one true faith.

In this Christian church He daily and richly forgives all my sins and the sins of all believers.

On the Last Day He will raise me and all the dead, and give eternal life to me and all believers in Christ.

This is most certainly true.

The Lord's Prayer

Our Father who art in heaven, hallowed be Thy name, Thy kingdom come, Thy will be done, on earth as it is in heaven. Give us this day our daily bread; and forgive us our trespasses as we forgive those who trespass against us; and lead us not into temptation; but deliver us from evil.

For Thine is the kingdom and the power and the glory forever and ever. Amen.

The Introduction

Our Father who art in heaven.

Q. What does this mean?

A. With these words God tenderly invites us to believe that He is our true Father and that we are His true children, so that with all boldness and confidence we may ask Him as dear children ask their dear father.

THE FIRST PETITION
Hallowed be Thy name.

Q. *What does this mean?*

A. God's name is certainly holy in itself, but we pray in this petition that it may be kept holy among us also.

Q. *How is God's name kept holy?*

A. God's name is kept holy when the Word of God is taught in its truth and purity, and we, as the children of God, also lead holy lives according to it. Help us to do this, dear Father in heaven! But anyone who teaches or lives contrary to God's Word profanes the name of God among us. Protect us from this, heavenly Father!

THE SECOND PETITION
Thy kingdom come.

Q. *What does this mean?*

A. The kingdom of God certainly comes by itself without our prayer, but we pray in this petition that it may come to us also.

Q. *How does God's kingdom come?*

A. God's kingdom comes when our heavenly Father gives us His Holy Spirit, so that by His grace we believe His holy Word and lead godly lives here in time and there in eternity.

THE THIRD PETITION
Thy will be done on earth as it is in heaven.

Q. What does this mean?

A. The good and gracious will of God is done even without our prayer, but we pray in this petition that it may be done among us also.

Q. How is God's will done?

A. God's will is done when He breaks and hinders every evil plan and purpose of the devil, the world, and our sinful nature, which do not want us to hallow God's name or let His kingdom come; and when He strengthens and keeps us firm in His

Word and faith until we die. This is His good and gracious will.

THE FOURTH PETITION
Give us this day our daily bread.

Q. What does this mean?

A. God certainly gives daily bread to everyone without our prayers, even to all evil people, but we pray in this petition that God would lead us to realise this and to receive our daily bread with thanksgiving.

Q. What is meant by daily bread?

A. Daily bread includes everything that has to do with the support and needs of the body, such as food, drink, clothing, shoes, house, home, land, animals, money, goods, a devout husband or wife, devout children, devout workers, devout and faithful rulers, good government, good weather, peace, health, self-control, good repu- tation, good friends, faithful neighbours, and the like.

THE FIFTH PETITION

And forgive us our trespasses as we forgive those who trespass against us.

Q. What does this mean?

A. We pray in this petition that our Father in heaven would not look at our sins, or deny our prayer because of them. We are neither worthy of the things for which we pray, nor have we deserved them, but we ask that He would give them all to us by grace, for we daily sin much and surely deserve nothing but punishment. So we too will sincerely forgive and gladly do good to those who sin against us.

THE SIXTH PETITION

And lead us not into temptation.

Q. *What does this mean?*

A. God tempts no one. We pray in this petition that God would guard and keep us so that the devil, the world, and our sinful nature may not deceive us or mislead us into false belief, despair, and other great shame and vice. Although we are attacked by these things, we pray that we may finally overcome them and win the victory.

THE SEVENTH PETITION

But deliver us from evil.

Q. *What does this mean?*

A. We pray in this petition, in summary, that our Father in heaven would rescue us from every evil of body and soul, possessions and reputation, and finally, when our last hour comes, give us a blessed end, and graciously take us from this valley of sorrow to Himself in heaven.

THE CONCLUSION

For Thine is the kingdom and the power and the glory forever and ever.* Amen.

Q. *What does this mean?*

A. This means that I should be certain that these petitions are pleasing to our Father in heaven, and are heard by Him; for He Himself has commanded us to pray in this way and has promised to hear us. Amen, amen means "yes, yes, it shall be so."

*These words were not in Luther's Small Catechism.

THE SACRAMENT OF HOLY BAPTISM

THE HEAD OF THE FAMILY SHOULD TEACH IT IN A SIMPLE WAY TO HIS HOUSEHOLD.

FIRST

What is Baptism?

A. Baptism is not just plain water, but it is the water included in God's command and combined with God's word.

Q. *Which is that word of God?*

A. Christ our Lord says in the last chapter of Matthew: "Therefore go and make disciples of all nations, baptising them in the name of the Father and of the Son and of the Holy Spirit." —Matt. 28:19

SECOND

What benefits does Baptism give?

A. It works forgiveness of sins, rescues from death and the devil, and gives eternal salvation to all who believe this, as the words and promises of God declare.

Which are these words and promises of God?

A. Christ our Lord says in the last chapter of Mark: "Whoever believes and is baptised will be saved, but whoever does not believe will be condemned." —Mark 16:16

THIRD

How can water do such great things?

A. Certainly not just water, but the word of God in and with the water does these things, along with the faith which trusts this word of God in the water. For without God's word the water is plain water and no Baptism. But with the word of God it is a Baptism, that is, a life-giving water, rich in grace, and a washing of the new birth in the Holy Spirit, as St Paul says in Titus, chapter three—

"He saved us through the washing of rebirth and renewal by the Holy Spirit, whom He poured out on us generously through Jesus Christ our Saviour, so that, having been justified by His grace, we might become heirs having the hope of eternal life. This is a trustworthy saying." —Titus 3:5–8

FOURTH

What does such baptising with water indicate?

A. It indicates that the Old Adam in us should by daily contrition and repentance be drowned and die with all sins and evil desires, and that a new man should daily emerge and arise to live before God in righteousness and purity forever.

Where is this written?

A. St. Paul writes in Romans chapter six: "We were therefore buried with Him through baptism into death in order that, just as Christ was raised from the dead through the glory of the Father, we too may live a new life." —Rom. 6:4

CONFESSION

How Christians should be
taught to confess.

Q. What is Confession?

A. Confession has two parts—

First, that we confess our sins, and second, that we receive absolution, that is, forgiveness, from the pastor as from God Himself, not doubting, but firmly believing that by it our sins are forgiven before God in heaven.

Q. What sins should we confess?

A. Before God we should plead guilty of all sins, even those we are not aware of, as we do in the Lord's Prayer; but before the pastor we should confess only those sins which we know and feel in our hearts.

Q. Which are these?

A. Consider your place in life according to the Ten Commandments: Are you a father, mother, son, daughter, husband, wife, or worker? Have you been disobedient, unfaithful, or lazy? Have you been hot-tempered, rude, or quarrel-

some? Have you hurt someone by your words or
deeds? Have you stolen, been negligent, wasted
anything, or done any harm?

A SHORT FORM OF CONFESSION

(Luther intended the following form to serve
only as an example of private confession for
Christians of his time. For a contemporary form
of individual confession, see *Lutheran Worship*,
pp. 310–11.)

The penitent says—

*Dear confessor, I ask you please to hear my
confession and to pronounce forgiveness in order
to fulfil God's will.*

*I, a poor sinner, plead guilty before God of all
sins. In particular I confess before you that as a
servant, maid, etc., I, sad to say, serve my master
unfaithfully, for in this and that I have not done
what I was told to do. I have made him angry
and caused him to curse. I have been negligent
and allowed damage to be done. I have also been
offensive in words and deeds. I have quarrelled
with my peers. I have grumbled about the lady
of the house and cursed her. I am sorry for all of
this and I ask for grace. I want to do better.*

A master or lady of the house may say—

In particular I confess before you that I have not faithfully guided my children, servants, and wife to the glory of God. I have cursed. I have set a bad example by indecent words and deeds. I have hurt my neighbour and spoken evil of him. I have overcharged, sold inferior merchandise, and given less than was paid for.

(Let the penitent confess whatever else he has done against God's commandments and his own position.)

If, however, someone does not find himself burdened with these or greater sins, he should not trouble himself or search for or invent other sins, and thereby make confession a torture. Instead, he should mention one or two that he knows: In particular I confess that I have cursed; I have used improper words; I have neglected this or that, etc. Let that be enough.

But if you know of none at all (which is hardly possible), then mention none in particular, but receive the forgiveness upon the general confession which you make to God before the confessor.

Then the confessor shall say—

God be merciful to you and strengthen your faith. Amen.

Furthermore—

Do you believe that my forgiveness is God's forgiveness?

Yes, dear confessor.

Then let him, say—

Let it be done for you as you believe. And I, by the command of our Lord Jesus Christ, forgive you your sins in the name of the Father and of the Son and of the Holy Spirit. Amen. Go in peace.

(A confessor will know additional passages with which to comfort and to strengthen the faith of those who have great burdens of conscience or are sorrowful and distressed. This is intended only as a general form of confession.)

[Note: The following three questions were not likely composed by Luther himself nor were they included in his original catechism but they reflect his teaching and were included in subsequent editions of the catechism during his lifetime without his objection.]

Q. What is the Office of the Keys?

A. The Office of the Keys is that special authority which Christ has given to His church on earth to forgive the sins of repentant sinners, but to withhold forgiveness from the unrepentant as long as they do not repent.

Q. Where is this written?

A. This is what St. John the Evangelist writes in chapter twenty: The Lord Jesus breathed on His disciples and said, "Receive the Holy Spirit. If you forgive anyone his sins, they are forgiven; if you do not forgive them, they are not forgiven." (John 20:22–23)

Q. What do you believe according to these words?

A. I believe that when the called ministers of Christ deal with us by His divine command, in particular when they exclude openly unrepentant sinners from the Christian congregation and absolve those who repent of their sins and want to do better, this is just as valid and certain, even in heaven, as if Christ our dear Lord dealt with us Himself.

THE SACRAMENT
OF THE ALTAR

THE HEAD OF THE FAMILY SHOULD TEACH
IT IN A SIMPLE WAY TO HIS HOUSEHOLD.

Q. What is the Sacrament of the Altar?

A. It is the true body and blood of our Lord Jesus Christ under the bread and wine, instituted by Christ Himself for us Christians to eat and to drink.

Q. Where is this written?

A. The holy Evangelists Matthew, Mark, Luke, and St Paul write:

"Our Lord Jesus Christ, on the night when He was betrayed, took bread, and when He had given thanks, He broke it and gave it to the disciples and said: 'Take, eat; this is My body, which is given for you. This do in remembrance of Me.'

In the same way also He took the cup after supper, and when He had given thanks, He gave it to them, saying, 'Drink of it, all of you; this cup is the new testament in My blood, which is shed for you for the forgiveness of sins. This do, as often as you drink it, in remembrance of Me.' "

Q. What is the benefit of this eating and drinking?

A. These words, "Given and shed for you for the forgiveness of sins," show us that in the Sacrament forgiveness of sins, life, and salvation are given us through these words. For where there is forgiveness of sins, there is also life and salvation.

Q. How can bodily eating and drinking do such great things?

A. Certainly not just eating and drinking do these things, but the words written here: "Given and shed for you for the forgiveness of sins." These words, along with the bodily eating and drinking, are the main thing in the Sacrament. Whoever believes these words has exactly what they say: "forgiveness of sins."

Q. Who receives this sacrament worthily?

A. Fasting and bodily preparation are certainly fine outward training. But that person is truly worthy and well prepared who has faith in these words: "Given and shed for you for the forgiveness of sins."

But anyone who does not believe these words or doubts them is unworthy and unprepared, for the words "for you" require all hearts to believe.

SECTION 2

DAILY PRAYERS

HOW THE HEAD OF THE HOUSEHOLD SHOULD TEACH HIS HOUSEHOLD TO PRAY MORNINGS AND EVENINGS.

Morning Prayer

In the morning when you get up, make the sign of the holy cross and say:

In the name of the Father and of the Son and of the Holy Spirit. Amen.

Then, kneeling or standing, repeat the Creed and the Lord's Prayer. If you choose, you may also say this little prayer—

I thank You, my heavenly Father, through Jesus Christ, Your dear Son, that You have kept me this night from all harm and danger; and I pray that You would keep me this day also from sin and every evil, that all my doings and life may please You. For into Your hands I commend myself, my body and soul, and all things. Let Your holy angel be with me, that the evil foe may have no power over me. Amen.

Then go joyfully to your work, singing a hymn, like that of the Ten Commandments, or whatever your devotion may suggest.

Evening Prayer

In the evening when you go to bed, make the sign of the holy cross and say—

In the name of the Father and of the Son and of the Holy Spirit. Amen.

Then kneeling or standing, repeat the Creed and the Lord's Prayer. If you choose, you may also say this little prayer—

I thank You, my heavenly Father, through Jesus Christ, Your dear Son, that You have graciously kept me this day; and I pray that You would forgive me all my sins where I have done wrong, and graciously keep me this night. For into Your hands I commend myself, my body and soul, and all things. Let Your holy angel be with me, that the evil foe may have no power over me. Amen.

Then go to sleep at once and in good cheer.

GIVING THANKS

HOW THE HEAD OF HOUSEHOLD SHOULD TEACH HIS HOUSEHOLD TO ASK A BLESSING AND RETURN THANKS.

Asking a Blessing

The children and members of the household shall go to the table reverently, fold their hands, and say—

"The eyes of all look to You, (O Lord,) and You give them their food at the proper time. You open Your hand and satisfy the desires of every living thing." —Ps. 145:15– 16

Then shall be said the Lord's Prayer and the following—

Lord God, heavenly Father, bless us and these Your gifts which we receive from Your bountiful goodness, through Jesus Christ, our Lord. Amen.

Returning Thanks

Also, after eating, they shall, in like manner, reverently and with folded hands say—

Give thanks to the Lord, for He is good. His love endures forever. (He) gives food to every creature. He provides food for the cattle and for the young ravens when they call. His pleasure is not in the strength of the horse, nor His delight in the legs of a man; the Lord delights in those who fear Him, who put their hope in His unfailing love." —Ps. 136:1, 25; 147:9–11

Then shall be said the Lord's Prayer and the following—

We thank You, Lord God, heavenly Father, for all Your benefits, through Jesus Christ, our Lord, who lives and reigns with You and the Holy Spirit forever and ever. Amen.

SECTION 3

TABLE OF DUTIES

CERTAIN PASSAGES OF SCRIPTURE FOR VARIOUS
HOLY ORDERS AND POSITIONS, ADMONISHING THEM
ABOUT THEIR DUTIES AND RESPONSIBILITIES.

To Bishops, Pastors, and Preachers—

"The overseer must be above reproach, the husband of but one wife, temperate, self-controlled, respectable, hospitable, able to teach, not given to drunkenness, not violent but gentle, not quarrelsome, not a lover of money. He must manage his own family well and see that his children obey him with proper respect." —1 Tim. 3:2–4

"He must not be a recent convert, or he may become conceited and fall under the same judgment as the devil." —1 Tim. 3:6

"He must hold firmly to the trustworthy message as it has been taught, so that he can encourage others by sound doctrine and refute those who oppose it." —Titus 1:9

What the Hearers Owe Their Pastors

"The Lord has commanded that those who preach the gospel should receive their living from the gospel." —1 Cor. 9:14

Anyone who receives instruction in the word must share all good things with his instructor. Do not be deceived: God cannot be mocked. A man reaps what he sows. —Gal. 6:6– 7

"The elders who direct the affairs of the church well are worthy of double honour, especially those whose work is preaching and teaching. For the Scripture says, 'Do not muzzle the ox while it is treading out the grain,' and 'The worker deserves his wages.' " —1 Tim. 5:17–18

"We ask you, brothers, to respect those who work hard among you, who are over you in the Lord and who admonish you. Hold them in the highest regard in love because of their work. Live in peace with each other." —1 Thess. 5:12–13

"Obey your leaders and submit to their authority. They keep watch over you as men who must give an account. Obey them so that their work will be a joy, not a burden, for that would be of no advantage to you." —Heb. 13:17

Of Civil Government

"Everyone must submit himself to the governing authorities, for there is no authority except that which God has established. The authorities that exist have been established by

God. Consequently, he who rebels against the authority is rebelling against what God has instituted, and those who do so will bring judgment on themselves. For rulers hold no terror for those who do right, but for those who do wrong. Do you want to be free from fear of the one in authority? Then do what is right and he will commend you. For he is God's servant to do you good. But if you do wrong, be afraid, for he does not bear the sword for nothing. He is God's servant, an agent of wrath to bring punishment on the wrongdoer." —Rom. 13:1–4

Of Citizens

"Give to Caesar what is Caesar's, and to God what is God's." —Matt. 22:21

"It is necessary to submit to the authorities, not only because of possible punishment but also because of conscience. This is also why you pay taxes, for the authorities are God's servants, who give their full time to governing. Give everyone what you owe him: If you owe taxes, pay taxes; if revenue, then revenue; if respect, then respect; if honour, then honour." —Rom. 13:5–7

"I urge, then, first of all, that requests, prayers, intercession and thanksgiving be made for everyone–for kings and all those in authority, that we may live peaceful and quiet lives in all godliness and holiness. This is good, and pleases God our Savoir." —1 Tim. 2:1–3

"Remind the people to be subject to rulers and authorities, to be obedient, to be ready to do whatever is good." —Titus 3:1

"Submit yourselves for the Lord's sake to every authority instituted among men: whether to the king, as the supreme authority, or to governors, who are sent by him to punish those who do wrong and to commend those who do right." —1 Peter 2:13–14

To Husbands

"Husbands, in the same way be considerate as you live with your wives, and treat them with respect as the weaker partner and as heirs with you of the gracious gift of life, so that nothing will hinder your prayers." —1 Peter 3:7

"Husbands, love your wives and do not be harsh with them." —Col. 3:1

To Wives

"Wives, submit to your husbands as to the Lord." —Eph. 5:22

They were submissive to their own husbands, like Sarah, who obeyed Abraham and called him her master. You are her daughters if you do what is right and do not give way to fear. —1 Peter 3:5–6

To Parents

Fathers, do not exasperate your children; instead, bring them up in the training and instruction of the Lord. —Eph. 6:4

"Children, obey your parents in the Lord, for this is right. 'Honour your father and mother'—which is the first commandment with a promise—'that it may go well with you and that you may enjoy long life on the earth.'" —Eph. 6:1–3

To Workers of All Kinds

Slaves, obey your earthly masters with respect and fear, and with sincerity of heart, just as you would obey Christ. Obey them not only to win their favour when their eye is on you, but like slaves of Christ, doing the will of God from your heart. Serve wholeheartedly, as if you were serving the Lord, not men, because you know that the Lord will reward everyone for whatever good he does, whether he is slave or free. —Eph. 6:5–8

To Employers and Supervisors

Masters, treat your slaves in the same way. Do not threaten them, since you know that he who is both their Master and yours is in heaven, and there is no favouritism with Him. —Eph. 6:9

To Youth

Young men, in the same way be submissive to those who are older. All of you, clothe yourselves with humility toward one another, because, "God opposes the proud but gives grace to the humble." Humble yourselves, therefore, under God's mighty hand, that He may lift you up in due time. —1 Peter 5:5–6

To Widows

The widow who is really in need and left all alone puts her hope in God and continues night and day to pray and to ask God for help. But the widow who lives for pleasure is dead even while she lives. —1 Tim. 5:5–6

To Everyone

The commandments ... are summed up in this one rule: "Love your neighbour as yourself." —Rom. 13:9

I urge...that requests, prayers, intercession and thanksgiving be made for everyone. —1 Tim. 2:1

Let each his lesson learn with care, and all the household well shall fare.

SECTION 4

CHRISTIAN QUESTIONS WITH THEIR ANSWERS*

PREPARED BY DR. MARTIN LUTHER FOR THOSE WHO INTEND TO GO TO THE SACRAMENT

After confession and instruction in the Ten Commandments, the Creed, the Lord's Prayer, and the Sacraments of Baptism and the Lord's Supper, the pastor may ask, or Christians may ask themselves these questions—

1. Q. Do you believe that you are a sinner?
   A. Yes, I believe it. I am a sinner.

2. Q. How do you know this?
   A. From the Ten Commandments, which I have not kept.

3. Q. Are you sorry for your sins?
   A. Yes, I am sorry that I have sinned against God.

---

*The "Christian Questions with Their Answers," designating Luther as the author, first appeared in an edition of the Small Catechism in 1551.

4. Q. What have you deserved from God because of your sins?

A. His wrath and displeasure, temporal death, and eternal damnation. See Rom. 6:21, 23.

5. Q. Do you hope to be saved?

A. Yes, that is my hope.

6. Q. In whom then do you trust?

A. In my dear Lord Jesus Christ.

7. Q. Who is Christ?

A. The Son of God, true God and man.

8. Q. How many Gods are there?

A. Only one, but there are three persons: Father, Son, and Holy Spirit.

9. Q. What has Christ done for you that you trust in Him?

A. He died for me and shed His blood for me on the cross for the forgiveness of sins.

10. Q. Did the Father also die for you?

A. He did not. The Father is God only, as is the Holy Spirit; but the Son is both true God and true man. He died for me and shed His blood for me.

11. Q. How do you know this?

A. From the holy Gospel, from the words instituting the Sacrament, and by His body and blood given me as a pledge in the Sacrament.

12. Q. What are the words of institution?

A. "Our Lord Jesus Christ, on the night when He was betrayed, took bread, and when He had given thanks, He broke it and gave it to the disciples and said: 'Take eat; this is My body, which is given for you. This do in remembrance of Me.' In the same way also He took the cup after supper, and when He had given thanks, He gave it to them, saying: 'Drink of it, all of you; this cup is the new testament in My blood, which is shed for you for the forgiveness of sins. This do, as often as you drink it, in remembrance of Me.' "

13. Q. Do you believe, then, that the true body and blood of Christ are in the Sacrament?

A. Yes, I believe it.

14. Q. What convinces you to believe this?

A. The word of Christ: Take, eat, this is My body; drink of it, all of you, this is My blood.

15. Q. What should we do when we eat His body and drink His blood, and in this way receive His pledge?

A. We should remember and proclaim His death and the shedding of His blood, as He taught us: This do, as often as you drink it, in remembrance of Me.

16. Q. Why should we remember and proclaim His death?

A. First, so we may learn to believe that no creature could make satisfaction for our sins. Only Christ, true God and man, could do that. Second, so we may learn to be horrified by our sins, and to regard them as very serious. Third, so we may find joy and comfort in Christ alone, and through faith in Him be saved.

17. Q. What motivated Christ to die and make full payment for your sins?

His great love for His Father and for me and other sinners, as it is written in John 14; Romans 5; Galatians 2 and Ephesians 5.

18. Q. Finally, why do you wish to go to the Sacrament?

That I may learn to believe that Christ, out of great love, died for my sin, and also learn from Him to love God and my neighbour.

19. Q. What should admonish and encourage a Christian to receive the Sacrament frequently?

A. First, both the command and the promise of Christ the Lord. Second, his own pressing need, because of which the command, encouragement, and promise are given.

20. Q. But what should you do if you are not aware of this need and have no hunger and thirst for the Sacrament?

A. To such a person no better advice can be given than this: first, he should touch his body to see if he still has flesh and blood. Then he should believe what the Scriptures say of it in Galatians 5 and Romans 7.

Second, he should look around to see whether he is still in the world, and remember that there will be no lack of sin and trouble, as the Scriptures say in John 15–16 and in 1 John 2 and 5.

Third, he will certainly have the devil also around him, who with his lying and murdering day and night will let him have no peace, within or without, as the Scriptures picture him in John 8 and 16; 1 Peter 5; Ephesians 6; and 2 Timothy 2.

NOTE: These questions and answers are no child's play, but are drawn up with great earnestness of purpose by the venerable and devout Dr. Luther for both young and old. Let all pay attention and consider it a serious matter; for St. Paul writes to the Galatians in chapter six: "*Do not be deceived: God cannot be mocked.*"

THE MISSION OF GREAT CHRISTIAN BOOKS

The ministry of Great Christian Books was established to glorify The Lord Jesus Christ and to be used by Him to expand and edify the kingdom of God while we occupy and anticipate Christ's glorious return. Great Christian Books will seek to accomplish this mission by publishing Gospel literature which is biblically faithful, relevant, and practically applicable to many of the serious spiritual needs of mankind upon the beginning of this new millennium. To do so we will always seek to boldly incorporate the truths of Scripture, especially those which were largely articulated as a body of theology during the Protestant Reformation of the sixteenth century and ensuing years. We gladly join our voice in the proclamations of— Scripture Alone, Faith Alone, Grace Alone, Christ Alone, and God's Glory Alone!

Our ministry seeks the blessing of our God as we seek His face to both confirm and support our labors for Him. Our prayers for this work can be summarized by two verses from the Book of Psalms:

"...let the beauty of the LORD our God be upon us, And establish the work of our hands for us; Yes, establish the work of our hands." —Psalm 90:17

"Not unto us, O LORD, not unto us, but to your name give glory." —Psalm 115:1

Great Christian Books appreciates the financial support of anyone who shares our burden and vision for publishing literature which combines sound Bible doctrine and practical exhortation in an age when too few so-called "Christian" publications do the same. We thank you in advance for any assistance you can give us in our labors to fulfill this important mission. May God bless you.

For a catalog of other great
Christian books
contact us in
any of the following ways:

write us at:
Great Christian Books
160 37th Street
Lindenhurst, NY 11757

call us at:
631. 956. 0998

find us online:
www.greatchristianbooks.com

email us at:
mail@greatchristianbooks.com

68368179R00040

Made in the USA
Lexington, KY
09 October 2017